BIGFOOT

AND OTHER
MYSTERIOUS CREATURES

John Townsend

 Crabtree Publishing Company

www.crabtreebooks.com

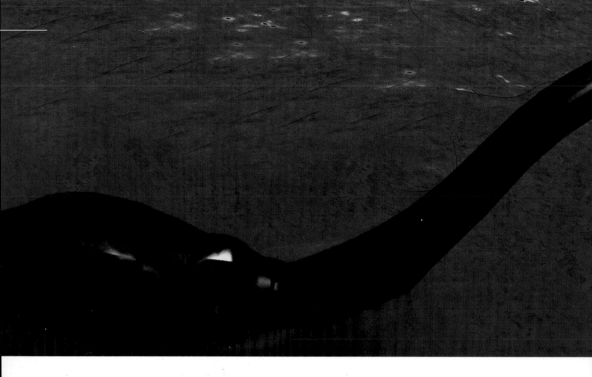

Crabtree Publishing Company

www.crabtreebooks.com   1-800-387-7650

Copyright © **2009 CRABTREE PUBLISHING COMPANY**. All rights reserved. No part of this publication may be reproduced, stored in a retrieval system or be transmitted in any form or by any means, electronic, mechanical, photocopying, recording, or otherwise, without the prior written permission of Crabtree Publishing Company.

**Published
in Canada
Crabtree Publishing**
616 Welland Ave.
St. Catharines, ON
L2M 5V6

**Published in the
United States
Crabtree Publishing**
PMB16A
350 Fifth Ave., Suite 3308
New York, NY 10118

Content development by Shakespeare Squared
www.ShakespeareSquared.com
First published in Great Britain in 2008 by ticktock Media Ltd,
2 Orchard Business Centre, North Farm Road,
Tunbridge Wells, Kent, TN2 3XF
Copyright © ticktock Entertainment Ltd 2008

Author: John Townsend
Project editor: Ruth Owen
Project designer: Sara Greasley
Photo research: Lizzie Knowles
Proofreaders: Robert Walker,
 Crystal Sikkens
Production coordinator:
 Katherine Kantor
Prepress technicians:
 Katherine Kantor, Ken Wright

With thanks to series
editors Honor Head
and Jean Coppendale.

Thank you to Lorraine
Petersen and the
members of nasen

Picture credits:
Alamy: Bryan & Cherry Alexander Photography: p. 17; Dale O'Dell:
 p. 1; Mary Evans Picture Library: p. 9; Alistair Siddons: p. 25
Corbis: Bettmann: p. 20, 21
Field Museum of Natural History: p. 11 (bottom)
Fortean Picture Library: John Sibbick: p. 24, 28 (bottom)
Getty Images: AFP: p. 19 (top); Keystone: p. 7 (top); Popperfoto:
 p. 19 (bottom); Topical Press Agency: p. 18, 29 (top right)
Simon Mendez: p. 22–23
Naturepl.com: Conrad Maufe: p. 10
James Powell: cover, p. 28 (top)
Rex Features: p. 26–27
Shutterstock: p. 2, 4, 5, 6–7, 11 (top), 12–13, 14–15, 16,
 28 (center), 29 (top left), 29 (bottom right)
The Natural History Museum, London: p. 23 (center)
Wikimedia Commons: Seo75: p. 31

Every effort has been made to trace copyright holders, and we apologize in
advance for any omissions. We would be pleased to insert the appropriate
acknowledgments in any subsequent edition of this publication.

Library and Archives Canada Cataloguing in Publication

Townsend, John, 1955-
  Bigfoot and other mysterious creatures / John Townsend.

(Crabtree contact)
Includes index.
ISBN 978-0-7787-3768-1 (bound).–ISBN 978-0-7787-3790-2 (pbk.)

  1. Monsters--Juvenile literature. I. Title. II. Series.

QL89.T69 2008   j001.944   C2008-905959-X

Library of Congress Cataloging-in-Publication Data

Townsend, John, 1955-
  Bigfoot and other mysterious creatures / John Townsend.
    p. cm. -- (Crabtree contact)
  Includes index.
  ISBN-13: 978-0-7787-3790-2 (pbk. : alk. paper)
  ISBN-10: 0-7787-3790-X (pbk. : alk. paper)
  ISBN-13: 978-0-7787-3768-1 (reinforced library binding : alk. paper)
  ISBN-10: 0-7787-3768-3 (reinforced library binding : alk. paper)
  1. Sasquatch--Juvenile literature. I. Title. II. Series.

QL89.2.S2T46 2009
001.944--dc22
                                                    2008039401

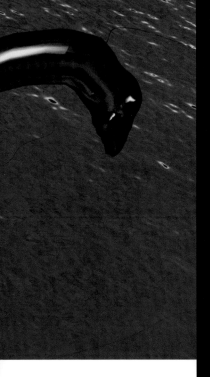

CONTENTS

SECRET BEASTS

Many places on Earth are **wilderness**.

Over half of Earth is covered with deep water.

Many people claim they have seen strange beasts in these places. In this book, you will read some of their stories.

Many scientists and explorers have tried to find these creatures — without success. Does this mean these strange beasts do not exist?

What do you believe?

It is time to take a closer look.

LOCH NESS MONSTER

For nearly 1,500 years, people have told stories of a secret beast in Scotland. People say the beast lives in a deep lake called Loch Ness.

In 1930, three young men were fishing on Loch Ness. Suddenly, a large creature swam toward their boat under the water.

The creature turned away about 980 feet (298 meters) from the boat. The fishermen were sure it was the Loch Ness Monster.

This famous photo of the monster was taken in 1934. However, it turned out to be a **hoax**. The monster was just a model!

In 1960, **eyewitness** Torquil MacLeod says he saw the Loch Ness Monster rise from the water.

He says the monster was from 50 to 65 feet (15 to 20 meters) long. It had a neck like an elephant's trunk.

Does Loch Ness hide a secret beast?

THE KRAKEN

For hundreds of years, sailors told stories of a giant sea monster. It was called the Kraken.

This picture was created in 1801. The artist created the drawing using descriptions from sailors who claimed to have seen the Kraken.

The Kraken was believed to reach up from the ocean and attack ships.

GIANT SQUID

Could there be giant, monster-like creatures living in the ocean?

Perhaps the Kraken was actually a giant squid. Giant squid live deep under the sea.

Giant squid

Tentacles

This giant squid was washed up on a beach. They can grow much larger than this, though!

A giant squid could cling to a boat
with the suckers on its tentacles.

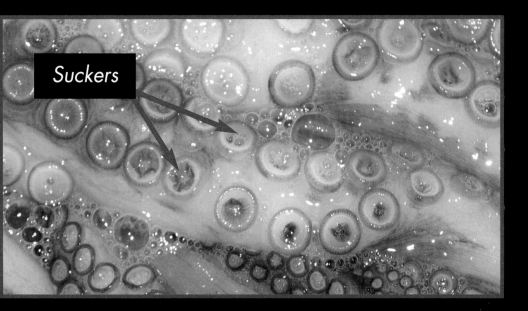

Suckers

Sailors say they have seen giant squid. They could
not measure them, but they **estimated** their length to
be from 60 to 65 feet (18 to 20 meters). The squids'
tentacles could be 18 feet (5.5 meters) long.

Perhaps some sea monsters were actually **oarfish**.
In 1996, this 24 foot (7.3 meters) oarfish was found
washed up on a beach in California.

TERATORNS

Six million years ago, giant birds called teratorns could be seen flying in the sky. A teratorns had a **wingspan** as big as an airplane!

Some people say they have seen teratorns in modern times.

In July 1977, people say they saw two giant birds in the sky above Lawndale, Illinois. The birds had wingspans of 26 feet (8 meters).

Suddenly, one of the birds swooped down. It lifted ten-year-old Marlon Lowe off the ground. Marlon's mother ran to help. She screamed and the bird dropped the boy.

Some people think Marlon was attacked by a teratorn.

Others say it was a large, modern-day bird. But no modern-day bird has such a large wingspan.

Could teratorns still exist today?

PREHISTORIC BEASTS

In prehistoric times, flying reptiles called pterosaurs ruled the skies.

For many years, people in Texas have reported seeing these same beasts.

In 1982, James Thompson was driving in Texas. Suddenly, something huge swooped down low over the road.

The creature had a wingspan of at least 6.5 feet (2 meters). There were no feathers on its wings — just skin.

When Thompson got home, he researched the creature in a book. The book showed the creature was a pterosaur!

Could prehistoric pterosaurs still exist today?

MOUNTAIN BEAST

For years, the people who live in the mountains of Tibet and Nepal have talked of the Yeti.

The Yeti has long dark hair.
It is 6.5 feet (2 meters) tall.
It walks like a human.

It also smells very bad!

In 2003, a girl in Nepal said she saw the Yeti.

The girl was looking after her **yaks**. The girls says the animals were attacked by the Yeti.

Yak

The Yeti was so strong it was able to kill the yaks with its bare hands.

The girl thought she was next. However, the beast disappeared back into the forest.

YETI EXPEDITION

Some people have seen Yeti footprints. Others have tried to find the Yeti.

In the 1930s, a team of men set off to climb **Mount Everest** in Nepal.

They saw huge footprints in the snow. Were they made by the Yeti?

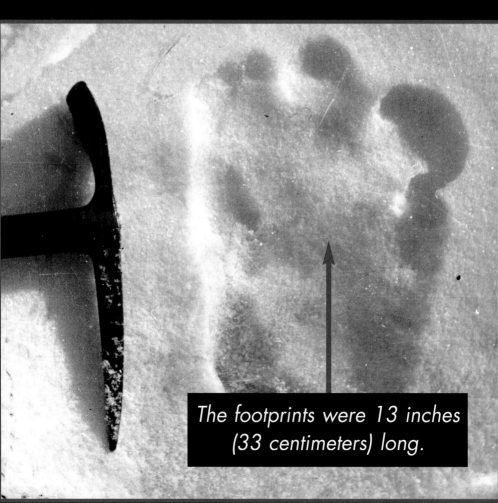

The footprints were 13 inches (33 centimeters) long.

In 1971, an **expedition** set off to try to find the Yeti. The expedition was led by a Japanese Yeti hunter named Takahashi.

Takahashi says one of his men saw the Yeti.

"It looked like a gorilla. It stood on its back legs, like a man. Its head was covered with long, thick hair. It was not a bear or a monkey."

Takahashi

Scalp

At a **monastery** in Nepal, the monks have a huge **scalp** of an unknown creature. They say it is the scalp of a Yeti.

BIGFOOT

In the wild places of North America, there are stories of a beast called Bigfoot.

A scientist holds up casts of Bigfoot prints.

In 1967, a man named Roger Patterson filmed a Bigfoot in northern California.

The Bigfoot was over 6.5 feet (2 meters) tall.

Patterson's film shows the creature walking toward the forest. It then turned and looked toward Patterson.

This is a photo from Patterson's film. Some scientists say the film shows an unknown animal. Others say it is a man wearing an ape suit!

GIANT APES

Adult man

Gigantopithecus

Giant apes once lived on Earth.

The giant ape Gigantopithecus was
10 feet (3 meters) tall. It lived until
half a million years ago.

Scientists know about this giant ape
because they have found **fossil** teeth.

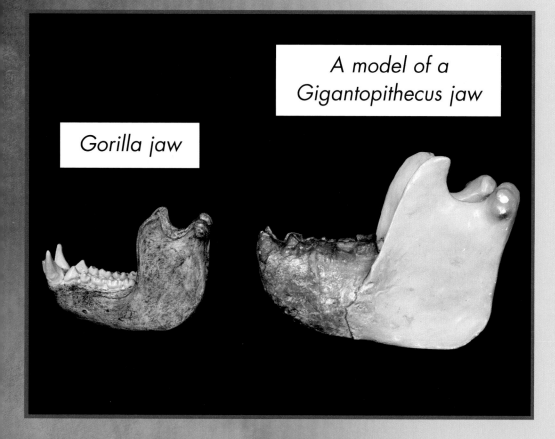

A model of a
Gigantopithecus jaw

Gorilla jaw

Could the creatures known as Bigfoot
and the Yeti be Gigantopithecus?

Could these giant apes
still be alive?

NIGHT KILLER

In parts of North America and South America, people say chupacabras attack goats, sheep, and chickens at night.

Some people believe chupacabras suck the animals' blood, and then leave them for dead.

What are chupacabras?

Some people say they were created in a science experiment. Then the killer beasts escaped from the science lab!

In 2006, Michelle O'Donnell of Maine, found an animal hit by a car. The animal was evil-looking with **fangs**. It looked like a dog. But not like any dog or wolf in the area!

Chupacabra

Spines

Fangs

Leathery skin

GIANT SNAKES

Man's body

This giant anaconda was caught in 1990. It was 33 feet (10 meters) long.

The snake had eaten a man!

Explorers in South American jungles say they have seen anacondas that are 98 feet (30 meters) long.

None that big have been caught — yet!

A WORLD OF MYSTERY

Stories of strange beasts have been told around the world for hundreds of years. Could some of these beasts still be out there?

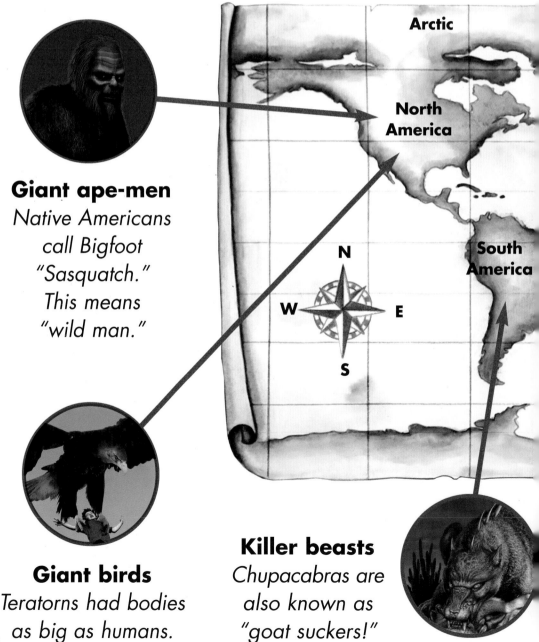

Giant ape-men
Native Americans call Bigfoot "Sasquatch." This means "wild man."

Arctic

North America

South America

N
W   E
S

Giant birds
Teratorns had bodies as big as humans.

Killer beasts
Chupacabras are also known as "goat suckers!"

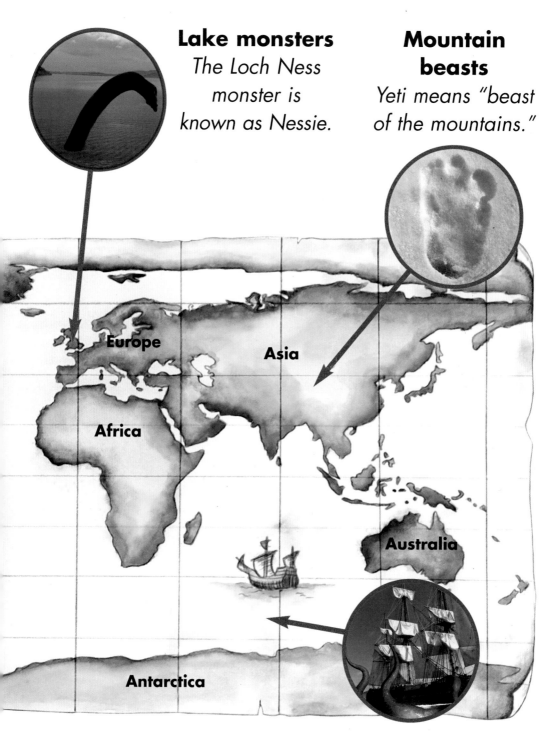

Lake monsters
The Loch Ness monster is known as Nessie.

Mountain beasts
Yeti means "beast of the mountains."

Europe

Asia

Africa

Australia

Antarctica

Perhaps there are even some beasts we don't know of yet. Keep looking.

Sea monsters
Some giant squid have eyes as big as dinner plates.

They may be closer than you think...

estimate To make a good guess using facts and eyewitness reports

expedition A long journey a group of people take to find out information

eyewitness A person who sees something happen

fang A long, sharp tooth

fossil A tooth or piece of bone that has turned into stone over millions of years

hoax A practical joke

monastery A place where monks and priests live and practice a religion

Mount Everest The highest mountain in the world. Everest is on the border of China and Nepal

oarfish A long fish with a thin, flat, ribbon-like body. People have reported seeing oarfish that were 56 feet (17 meters) long

reptile A cold-blooded animal with a backbone. Snakes, lizards, turtles, and crocodiles are all reptiles

scalp The skin that covers the top of the head, with the hair attached

tentacle A long body part that is used for touching and holding things

wilderness An area in which few people live that is still in its natural state

wingspan The measurement of a bird or plane's wings from wing tip to wing tip

yak A hairy, plant-eating, mountain animal. People in Nepal and Tibet keep yaks for their milk, meat, and skins

- For over 200 years, people have talked of "Chessie." They say this huge sea serpent lives around Chesapeake Bay on the east coast.

- In Australia, Aboriginal people talk of "Youree." It means "hairy man monster." The ape-man is also called "Yowie." Not many people have seen Yowie. People say it is very shy. They also say that Yowie stinks!

A statue of Yowie

SECRET BEASTS ONLINE

http://science.howstuffworks.com/bigfoot.htm
Learn about the history of Bigfoot

www.nessie.co.uk/
Read more about Nessie, the Loch Ness Monster

www.unmuseum.org/lostw.htm
Learn about other mysterious creatures

INDEX

A
anacondas 27
Australia 31

B
Bigfoot 20–21,
 23, 28, 31
birds 12–13, 28

C
Chessie 31
chupacabras
 24–25, 28

F
footprints 18, 20

G
giant squid
 10–11, 29
Gigantopithecus
 22–23

K
Kraken 8-9, 10

L
Loch Ness Monster
 6–7, 29, 31
Lowe, Marlon 12

M
MacLeod, Torquil 7

N
Nepal 16–17, 18–19
North America 20, 24, 28

O
O'Donnell, Michelle 24
oarfish 11

P
Patterson, Roger 20–21
pterosaurs 14–15

S
Scotland 6–7
sea monsters 8, 10–11,
 29, 31
South America 25, 27, 28

T
Takahashi 19
tentacles 10–11
teratorns 12–13, 28
Thompson, James 14–15
Tibet 16

W
wings 12, 15

Y
yaks 17
Yeti 16–17, 18–19,
 23, 29
Yowie 31

Printed in the U.S.A. - BG